ARCHITECTURE IN AMERICA

A PHOTOGRAPHIC HISTORY FROM
THE COLONIAL PERIOD TO THE PRESENT

BY WAYNE ANDREWS

INTRODUCTION BY RUSSELL LYNES

NEW YORK ATHENEUM PUBLISHERS 1960

FOR ALAN AND FRANCES BURNHAM

INTRODUCTION BY RUSSELL LYNES

It is a characteristic of the age in which we live that our visual pleasures are mainly two-dimensional. We are constantly exposed to the flat image—in books such as this, in magazines and newspapers, on billboards, in movies, and on the television screen. Picture galleries are more popular than sculpture galleries, a stage framed in a proscenium more popular than theatre-in-the-round. In what we are half-pleased to call the Space Age it sometimes seems that we prefer the two-dimensional illusion of space to space itself, and by and large we are often more comfortable looking at pictures of objects than at objects themselves.

The resources of the camera are endless; there is no man-made object in the world that hasn't been photographed or couldn't be, and this has made us lazy. We have unlimited opportunities for visual tasting and comparison, as Malraux has pointed out, such as no previous age ever had. As a result we have let tasting become a substitute for the more nourishing process of devouring. We have come to depend on the photographer to channel our vision, to fix it, focus it, frame it, and to eliminate what might distract us. He has relieved us of the necessity of having to select for ourselves; most of our visual experiences today have been deep-frozen by a lens.

Of all the visual arts (Geoffrey Scott called it "the most complicated of the arts") architecture has in some ways suffered most from the camera. It has become the creature of meaningless, if sometimes spectacular, camera angles and of filters that falsify its quality by exaggeration. But a building is not, as so many photographers seem to think, a subject for an "art" print. It is an object to be walked around and through, to be lived in and worked in. It is a complex structure that displaces air as a ship displaces water, and the spaces that a building contains are as individual as the shapes of the persons it houses. Because people are used to looking at architecture in photographs (indeed, most people are more likely than not to walk by an interesting building and see only the pavement in front of them), architecture is an art on which most of us exercise our taste and not our judgment. We look at style but not at structure; we see the detail but not the building (or sometimes, especially with modern buildings, we fail to notice the detail); we learn from photographs to recognize the handwriting of a period, its fashionable flourishes and eccentricities, but we cannot read what the handwriting says.

It might be more appropriate if this book were called *An Invitation to American Architecture*, for Wayne Andrews knows that even the most expert and honest photograph of a building can be no more than an invitation to it. But what an enticing and illuminating invitation this book is. As his own distinguished photographs immediately demonstrate, Wayne Andrews is a man who has walked through and around the buildings he has been at such pains over so many years to record. He has met the people (in fact or in history) who have built them and the people who have lived in them, for, as he wrote in *Architecture, Ambition and Americans* (1955), "I happen to believe that architectural history is only half told when the neatest analysis is made of the designs under consideration. I think that both client and architect are likely to be interesting individuals, and how the client was persuaded is a story worth hearing." To Wayne Andrews architecture is a personal art, and yet it is the least private of the arts: it exposes both the inspiration of its designer and the aspirations of its owner to public and, hopefully, permanent view.

Wayne Andrews does not say in this book, "Come look at my photographs." He says, "Come let me show you some of the buildings I have seen, enjoyed, and captured." There is a difference. This book is an enthusiastic tour of American architecture from the seventeenth century to 1959, enthusiastic rather than methodically conscientious, though Wayne Andrews' conscientiousness as a recorder of our architecture is not even remotely approached by any other photographer. This is a book of personal enjoyment, of delight in the architects' inventiveness, vision, and ingenuity with both materials and clients. It delights in social changes and the ways in which private and public aspirations exemplify themselves in marble and mortar, steel and glass, shingle and fieldstone. It is a reflecting pool for our social, political, and religious façade. It is, at the same time, a history of American architecture without in any sense being a compendium of our building. The academic historians of architecture will, I have no doubt, be saddened by the omission of some buildings they would expect to find here, just as the academic purists will be alarmed by some that they do. They may be worried, for example, by the amount of space given to the Romantic era and the once-over-lightly of the Colonial period. They may question the fact that there are no buildings by Cass Gilbert or by Raymond Hood or by Edward Stone, depending on their personal predilections or their individual reading of the historical record.

But the scheme and the sense of American architecture are here with the light of personal pleasure to illuminate them. Furthermore, there is evidence in Wayne Andrews' selection that the winds of taste are shifting, that some buildings which were a source of embarrassment a few years or a few decades ago have become, if not exactly respectable as art, at least recognizable for the energy and inventiveness of their design. We no longer need to squirm in our Eames chairs at the thought of Hunt's "cottage" for Mrs. Vanderbilt at Newport, "The Breakers," or at the befringed Gothic revival houses of A. J. Davis, as misguided attempts to make Americans into a falsely romantic image of themselves. (We should, however, be deeply embarrassed that Davis' beautiful Harral house in Bridgeport was permitted to be razed just a few years ago, an irreparable loss.) We can be proud, as Wayne Andrews obviously is, that the reputations of Sullivan and Richardson grow more lustrous with every year and that we have long since got beyond the point where we feel we must look over our shoulders to Europe for approval of our attempts at aesthetic expression.

No one, I believe, can turn over the pages of these photographs or read the succinct captions without a strong sense of the adventurousness of our architects and their clients. Even when our architecture was being derivative of fashionable European styles, it had, as these photographs so clearly demonstrate, a kind of gusto and self-assurance that was distinctly American. When it finally kicked over its European traces, it set a pace that the architecture of the rest of the world has followed, though the rest of the world was quicker to see what we had done to liberate an ancient art than we were.

It is, perhaps, too obvious to point out that in an age of mass production when so many things look so exactly like other things, and when so many of our architects have flirted with the modern spirit by filling our cities with almost indistinguishable glass boxes, that the individuality, extravagance, and energy of the 19th century and the first flowering of luxury in the 18th century have such a strong appeal for many of us, as they so obviously have for Wayne Andrews. There is not a banal building or a stereotype in this book, though there are a good many prototypes. This is a record of free spirits by a man whose eye is personal and penetrating, who delights in the inventive and the adventurous, who has no patience with clichés or dogmas, and who is, indeed, a free spirit himself.

PREFACE

Architecture in America is a photographic survey from the colonial period to the present. Like most surveys, it is far from definitive. Like most surveys, it is biassed. My bias will be evident to anyone who scans the captions or ponders the number of pages devoted to one architect in preference to another. For example, Frank Lloyd Wright is assigned twenty-four pages, or approximately one-seventh of the available space. The firm of McKim, Mead & White (in my opinion second in importance) is given fifteen pages, or second place. Not everyone will agree with my emphasis. I fail to see why everyone should.

Although this book is the record of twenty years work in the District of Columbia and forty five states, there are omissions which I regret. Benjamin Henry Latrobe is not represented, neither is the firm of Burnham & Root, nor the late Albert Kahn. In self-defence I might point out that much of the best of Latrobe's work (aside from the Capitol) has been destroyed, and that the gloom of the Loop makes it difficult for anyone not living in Chicago to find the perfect day for the Burnham & Root skyscrapers still standing. I should have liked to photograph Kahn's Half-Ton Truck plant for Dodge, but the Chrysler Corporation with great courtesy made plain that the building could not be taken for security reasons. I should add that I have purposely omitted Mount Vernon, the White House, and the Capitol, since they are familiar sights to all Americans.

In my judgment a good photograph is *not* a record of a building. It is an invitation to the beholder to go and see the building for himself. For this reason I have tried to take pictures from viewpoints normally available to the visitor.

This book would have been inconceivable without the complete co-operation of Compo Photo Service, who prepared all the prints. I am more than grateful to Richard I. Schuler of Compo, and to his associates Ernest Pile and Benjamin Morales.

Finally, I am indebted to Harry Ford of Atheneum, who designed this book with such care, and most of all to Simon Michael Bessie, who was the first to think of *Architecture in America.*

WAYNE ANDREWS

CONTENTS

San Estévan, Ácoma, New Mexico, 1642?(architect unknown).
This Franciscan mission, atop a 357-foot mesa, was the site of Willa
Cather's novel Death Comes for the Archbishop.

Nuestra Señora de la Asunción, Zia Pueblo, New Mexico, 1692 (architect unknown).
San Xavier del Bac, Tucson, Arizona, 1784–97 (architect unknown).
Like Nuestra Señora de la Asunción, San Xavier was built by Franciscans, but was unusually lavish.

San Francisco de Taos, Ranchos de Taos, New Mexico, c. 1772(architect unknown).
This too was a Franciscan mission.

ABOVE: *Saint Michael's Church, Charleston, South Carolina, 1761 (architect unknown).* BELOW: *Drayton Hall near Charleston, South Carolina, c. 1738 (architect unknown). Saint Michael's was one of the rare imposing churches of the colonial period. Drayton Hall was the seat of John Drayton, a native of Barbadoes who became one of the members of the Governor's Council.*

Residence of Miles Brewton, Charleston, South Carolina, c. 1769(architect unknown). The earnest New England patriot Josiah Quincy, Jr., who called on Brewton in 1773, was dismayed by the luxury of this town house, the finest in Charleston. Said Quincy of the Charleston aristocracy: "The gentlemen are mostly men of the turf and gamesters. Political inquiries and philosophical disquisitions are too laborious for them; they have no great passion for to shine and blaze in the forum or a senate."

In all likelihood we shall never know the names of the contrivers of most of our colonial buildings. Professional architects were unheard of until the late eighteenth century. The influence of the Italian Renaissance, carried to England by Inigo Jones and his successors, pervaded the colonies in the eighteenth century. The oustanding town and country houses—and possibly even an occasional church—were probably planned by enlightened men of leisure. With a book or two of plates of the latest architecture from Great Britain at his elbow, a dilettante (often the owner of an estate) could please himself and his descendants.

COLONIAL SOUTH CAROLINA

Exterior and interior of Saint James Church, Goose Creek, South Carolina, 1711 c.—interior c. 1790? (architect unknown). Here may be found the memorial to Ralph Izard, the only elegant expatriate of colonial times. A connoisseur of baroque and rococo music, he was disappointed in Italy when he found no music there to compare with that of Johann Christian Bach.

COLONIAL VIRGINIA

Westover, Residence of William Byrd II, Charles City County, Virginia, c. 1730 (architect unknown).

The grandson of a London goldsmith, William Byrd II sometimes forgot that he was the descendant of a tradesman. "Luxury," he once wrote his factor in England, "is bad enough amongst people of quality, but when it gets among that order of men that stand behind counters, they must turn cheats and pickpockets to get it, and then the Lord have mercy on those who are obliged to trust to their honesty." Carter Burwell was the grandson of Robert "King" Carter, the first great real estate speculator in the New World.

Carter's Grove, Residence of Carter Burwell, James City County, Virginia, c. 1751–53 (architect unknown).

Stratford, Residence of Thomas Lee, Westmoreland County, Virginia, c. 1725 (architect unknown). In this—the most imposing of all colonial houses still intact—was born Thomas Lee's descendant Robert E. Lee.

OPPOSITE ABOVE: *The Governor's Palace, Williamsburg, Virginia, 1706–20 (architect unknown).* BELOW: *The Capitol, Williamsburg, Virginia, 1751–53 (architect unknown). Both were restored by the generosity of John D. Rockefeller, Jr., 1928–34.*

9

Christ Church, Lancaster County, Virginia, 1732(architect unknown). Here was buried Robert "King" Carter, founder of the Carter dynasty. Shirley was built for one of his descendants; so was Carter's Grove.

OPPOSITE ABOVE: *Shirley, Charles City County, Virginia, c. 1769 (architect unknown).* BELOW: *Mount Airy, Richmond County, Virginia, c. 1758(architect unknown). The mother of Robert E. Lee was born at Shirley. Mount Airy was the home of John Tayloe, who kept one of the few private race tracks in colonial America.*

ABOVE: *Exterior of Gunston Hall, Lorton, Virginia, 1755 (architect unknown).* BELOW: *View of doorway at Gunston Hall. The interiors of Gunston Hall, the home of George Mason, who fought for the Bill of Rights, were designed by William Buckland, an indentured servant turned architect in the New World. By architect, we mean a man who makes plans for others to execute.*

COLONIAL
MARYLAND

ABOVE: *Hammond-Harwood house,
Annapolis, Maryland, 1770–74
(William Buckland).* BELOW:
*Interior of dining-room, Hammond-
Harwood house. This was the
greatest achievement of architect
William Buckland.*

13

The Saron or Sister House of The Cloister, Ephrata, Pennsylvania, 1741 (architect unknown). Built for the celibate sisterhood and celibate brotherhood of voluntarily divorced couples who joined the Society of the Solitary, the sect founded by the German mystic Johann Konrad Beissel. This was soon devoted uniquely to the needs of the sisterhood.

ABOVE: *Mount Pleasant, Philadelphia, Pennsylvania, 1761–62 (architect unknown)*.
BELOW: *Cliveden, Philadelphia, Pennsylvania, 1761 (architect unknown). These are the most eloquent examples extant of the wealth of Philadelphia when it was the second biggest city of the British Empire. The former was the home of the privateer James MacPherson, the latter of Chief Justice Benjamin Chew.*

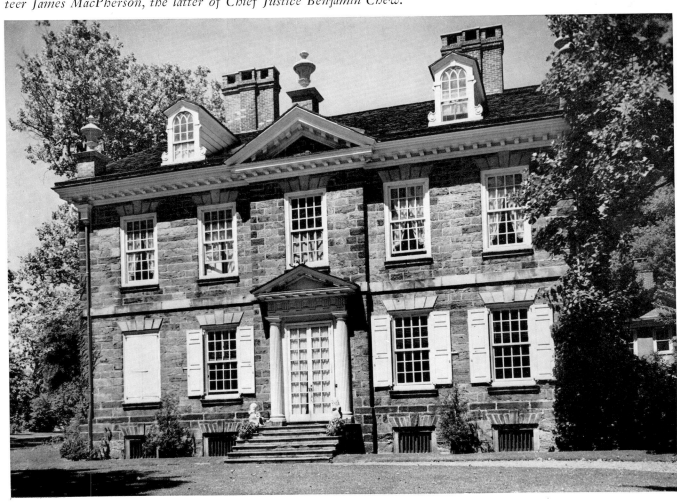

Residence of Parson Joseph Capen, Topsfield, Massachusetts, c. 1683 (architect unknown). This is probably the finest remaining example of 17th century American domestic architecture. The model for such a frame house could easily have been found in the countryside of 17th century England.

ABOVE: *Doorway, Residence of Samuel Porter, Hadley, Massachusetts, c. 1757 (architect unknown).* BELOW: *Rocky Hill Meeting House, Amesbury, Massachusetts, 1785 (architect unknown). The broken pediment of the Porter house at Hadley is typical of the attempts at elegance in the Connecticut Valley prior to the Revolution. The Rocky Hill Meeting House—an oblong without a tower—is characteristic of the austere houses of worship of those who broke away from the Church of England.*

OPPOSITE: *Christ Church, Cambridge, Massachusetts, 1761 (Peter Harrison).* ABOVE: *Interior. Harrison was the first American architect—that is, the first man to design buildings for others to erect.*

Redwood Library, Newport, Rhode Island, 1748 (Peter Harrison).

Residence of Zenas Cowles, Farmington, Connecticut, 1780 (William Sprats).

*Residence of Julius Deming, Litchfield, Connecticut, 1790–93 (William Sprats).
Though completed after the ratification of the Constitution, this house properly
belongs in any survey of the colonial architecture of New England.*

OPPOSITE: *Capitol, Richmond, Virginia, 1785–92 (Thomas Jefferson). This, the first example in the modern world of a public building in the temple style, was modeled after the Maison Carrée in Nîmes. Reverence for the architecture of ancient Rome was widespread at the beginning of the 19th century.*

In this time our government was founded and consolidated and Washington, D.C. was laid out and built up. This was also the time in which American architecture came into its own.

The Federal Period was remarkable for the number of architects from abroad who settled in the United States and raised our standards. Thanks to their presence, the professional architect was no longer an oddity. From the West Indies came William Thornton, who provided the first design for the U.S. Capitol. From Ireland came James Hoban, who not only worked on the Capitol but designed the White House. From France came Pierre-Charles L'Enfant, who gave us the plan of Washington, Etienne-Sulpice Hallet, who collaborated on the Capitol, Maximilien Godefroy, who created the First Unitarian Church in Baltimore, Joseph-François Mangin, who joined the native American John McComb, Jr., on the New York City Hall, and Joseph-Jacques Ramée, who laid out Union College. From England came William Jay, who brightened Savannah, George Hadfield, who superintended the U.S. Capitol, and most important of all the architects of the Federal Period, Benjamin Henry Latrobe. Most of Latrobe's private houses have been destroyed, but his genius is not likely to be forgotten since he was the major architect in the building of the U.S. Capitol.

Of our native architects Thomas Jefferson was easily the most distinguished. There was also Charles Bulfinch, who is known to have attacked the traditional colonial floor plan of a central hall with two rooms on each side by building a house—now destroyed—which boasted an elliptical salon, a French innovation. Then there was Samuel McIntire, the carver-turned-architect of Salem, Massachusetts, whose square frame houses concealed rather elaborate interiors modeled after those of the brothers Adam in England. Finally Asher Benjamin, who published the first American builders' guides, could scarcely be overlooked.

ABOVE: *Monticello, Residence of Thomas Jefferson, Charlottesville, Virginia, 1770–1809 (Thomas Jefferson). Jefferson modeled his own house after the villas erected in 18th century England by the Earl of Burlington, who—like Jefferson— was especially fond of the work of the 16th century Italian Andrea Palladio. But Jefferson was shrewder than Burlington when it came to adapting Palladio to a non-Italian site.* BELOW: *Bremo, Residence of John Hartwell Cocke, Fluvanna County, Virginia, 1815–19(architect unknown). Cocke himself may have been the designer of this Jeffersonian country seat.*

24

THE FEDERAL PERIOD

ABOVE: *The Octagon, Residence of John Tayloe, Washington, D.C., 1800 (William Thornton). This town house by the designer of the first plan for the U.S. Capitol is in 1960 the headquarters of the American Institute of Architects.*
BELOW: *Rotunda, University of Virginia, Charlottesville, Virginia, 1822–26 (Thomas Jefferson). The rotunda dominating this distinguished campus by Jefferson was later restored by Stanford White after a fire.*

ABOVE: *Residence of Nathaniel Russell, Charleston, South Carolina, c. 1811 (architect unknown).* BELOW: *Drawing Room.*

THE FEDERAL PERIOD

ABOVE: *Gardener's Cottage, and* BELOW: *Residence of Joseph Manigault, Charleston, South Carolina, 1790–97 (Gabriel Manigault). There were gentlemen of leisure who practiced architecture in the Federal Period; one of these was the Charlestonian Gabriel Manigault, son-in-law of Ralph Izard. In the gardener's cottage for his brother Joseph, Gabriel Manigault may have taken as his model one of the temples in the gardens of Stowe in 18th century England. The delicate interior of the house may have been inspired by the work of the brothers Adam.*

Living Room, Residence of Joseph Manigault, Charleston, South Carolina, 1790–97 (Gabriel Manigault).

*Residence of William Scarborough, Savannah, Georgia, c. 1818
(William Jay). One of the truly talented architects of the South in
the Federal Period was the Englishman William Jay, who brought
to Savannah something of the elegance of Regency England.*

*Hyde Hall, Residence of George Hyde Clark, Cooperstown, New York, 1811–13
(Edward Hooker). Edward Hooker of Schenectady, the designer of the old Capitol and City Hall at Albany (since replaced) fashioned this villa for an Englishman who was one of the great landholders of this section of New York State.*

City Hall, New York City, 1811 (Joseph-François Mangin & John McComb, Jr.).
The elegant Louis XVI façade is obviously the contribution of Mangin.

Gore Place and Living Room, Residence of Christopher Gore, Waltham, Massachusetts, 1797–1804 (architect unknown). Although no one knows who designed this country seat for Governor Gore, the influence of Charles Bulfinch is unmistakable, for he was the one who introduced elliptical rooms in Federal New England.

THE FEDERAL PERIOD

Christ Church, Lancaster, Massachusetts, 1816 (Charles Bulfinch).
One of the remarkable churches by the most remarkable architect of
New England in the Federal Period.

First Congregational Church, Bennington, Vermont, 1806 (Lavius Fillmore). Although Fillmore was the architect of this church, he based his design on Plate 33 in Asher Benjamin's The Country Builder's Assistant. *Benjamin was the first American to publish builders' guides for American use.*

Gardiner-White-Pingree house, Salem, Massachusetts, 1810 (Samuel McIntire). This is a typical example of the work of the carver-turned-architect who left his imprint on Salem in the Federal Period.

Residence of Joseph Nightingale, Providence, Rhode Island, 1792(Caleb Ormsbee).

Residence of John Brown, Providence, Rhode Island, 1785(Joseph Brown). Providence in the Federal Period was one of the great architectural centers. A leading architect was Joseph Brown of the famous family of merchants; he designed this imposing mansion for his brother John.

35

Linden Place, Residence of George DeWolf, Bristol, Rhode Island, 1810(Russell Warren).

Residence of John Peirce, Portsmouth, New Hampshire, 1800 (architect unknown).

THE ROMANTIC ERA 1820–1860

It was in the Romantic Era that the battle for modern architecture began. This may seem strange. The Romantic Era was the heyday of the Greek, the Gothic and many other revivals, and we all know that nothing seems more old-fashioned today than a return to the past, no matter what the excuse.

At first glance the romantics may seem innocent enough. Critics and architects alike, they were anxious to exploit the poetry of time past. But this was in the end a dangerous preoccupation. Though we may smile at the notion of a businessman traveling into the Middle Ages once he retired to his Gothic villa, this was the way the prestige of the Renaissance, which had held both England and 18th century America in its spell, was undermined. Once the prestige of the masters of the Renaissance was shattered, buildings could be planned, not to fit pre-conceived ideas of symmetry, but the desires of a growing family or business. The Gothic, by far the most vigorous of the romantic revivals, marked the end of the supremacy of the formal plan of the 18th century and the first step toward the planning-for-convenience of the 20th. Furthermore, once Gothic architecture was invested with mystery by the romantics, scholars could not help discovering the engineering achievements of the Middle Ages. And so the romantics reminded their descendants that architecture could be an adventure in engineering.

Both the Greek and the Gothic Revivals were of English origin. The former was launched in 1762 with the publication of Stuart and Revett's *Antiquities of Athens;* the latter was encouraged by the beginning of Horace Walpole's Gothic castle "Strawberry Hill" in 1750. It was Latrobe who introduced the Greek Revival—with the Bank of Pennsylvania (1799)—and the Gothic Revival—with William Crammond's house, Philadelphia (1799). These were too advanced for the taste of the Federal Period. But Latrobe's daring was an incentive to the romantics.

OPPOSITE ABOVE: *County Record (or Fireproof) Building, Charleston, South Carolina, 1822–27 (Robert Mills).* BELOW: *Bethesda Presbyterian Church, Camden, South Carolina, 1820 (Robert Mills). Mills, who studied under Latrobe after being encouraged by Jefferson, was the first American to be trained for the architectural profession. He later designed the Washington Monuments in Baltimore and Washington.*

ABOVE *and* OPPOSITE ABOVE: *Residence of H. K. Harral, Bridgeport, Connecticut,*
1846 (Alexander Jackson Davis). BELOW: *Interior of a bedroom. This Gothic*
villa, one of the greatest achievements of America's greatest romantic architect,
was willed to the city of Bridgeport by the last owner, Archer C. Wheeler. In
1958 the Harral-Wheeler house was destroyed during the administration of
Mayor Samuel Tedesco. The public protest was widespread, but futile.

Capitol, Raleigh, North Carolina, 1831–33 (Town, Davis & Paton). Davis, who was nothing if not versatile, was as expert at the Greek Revival as at the Gothic. He collaborated on this, the most distinguished of all our state capitols, with Ithiel Town and David Paton.

Residence of Henry Delamater, Rhinebeck, New York, 1844(Alexander Jackson Davis). This Gothic cottage was designed for the local banker and built by local carpenters without the architect's supervision. His practice was so extensive that he could supervise only the most elaborate commissions.

Entrance Lodge to Llewellyn Park, West Orange, New Jersey, c. 1857 (Alexander Jackson Davis). Davis made his own home in Llewellyn Park, a prize example of romantic planning laid out to suit the benevolent wholesale druggist Llewellyn Haskell.

Residence of W. J. Rotch, New Bedford, Massachusetts, 1850 (Alexander Jackson Davis).

ABOVE: *Residence of E. C. Litchfield, Brooklyn, New York, 1854(Alexander Jackson Davis).* BELOW: *La Grange Terrace, New York City, 1832 (Town & Davis & J. H. Dakin). The Litchfield mansion—built for the promoter of the first railroad to tie Chicago with the east coast—shows Davis's talent at designing a villa in the "Italian" manner. No reference to the Renaissance was intended; this is still another romantic attempt to introduce asymmetry into the American home. La Grange Terrace, built in collaboration with Ithiel Town and James Harrison Dakin (who later created the Gothic capitol of Louisiana at Baton Rouge) again proves Davis's sure hand in the Grecian manner.*

45

Belmead, Residence of Philip St. George Cocke, Powhatan County, Virginia, 1845 (Alexander Jackson Davis). This Gothic villa (converted into a Roman Catholic School for Negroes) was designed for General Cocke, who took his own life in the Civil War, but not before he had helped Davis create the Gothic buildings for the Virginia Military Institute at Lexington.

46

THE ROMANTIC ERA

ABOVE: *New York Yacht Club, Hoboken, New Jersey, 1846 (Alexander Jackson Davis).* BELOW: *Residence of C. B. Sedgwick, Syracuse, New York, 1845 (Alexander Jackson Davis). The Gothic clubhouse, which had been moved to Glen Cove, Long Island, when this picture was taken, has since been transplanted to Mystic, Connecticut. The Gothic house in Syracuse is serving, as of the moment of writing, as the headquarters of an advertising agency.*

Grace Church, New York City, 1846 (James Renwick, Jr.). One of the finest Gothic churches of the Romantic Era, this was designed by the only American architect to keep two steam yachts, one for cruising off the Florida coast, the other for voyages farther from home. He was only twenty-eight when this commission was completed. His mother was a Brevoort. His wife was an Aspinwall.

48

THE ROMANTIC ERA

Residence of C. T. Longstreet, Syracuse, New York, 1851 (James Renwick, Jr.). The Gothic castle at Syracuse (recently destroyed by Syracuse University) was designed for the first American to ship ready-made suits to the west coast.

Rectory, Grace Church, New York City, 1847 (James Renwick, Jr.).

Trinity Church, New York City, 1846 (Richard Upjohn). This Gothic structure, the greatest of all the churches of the Romantic Era, was designed by a high-minded native of England who had doubts about building churches for other than Episcopalians, and always insisted on what was proper for ritual use. He once de-signed a Presbyterian church. A rival observed that "he did it conscientiously, upon the ground that Presbyterians were not entitled to architecture."

*Saint Mary's Church and Interior,
Burlington, New Jersey, 1846–54
(Richard Upjohn). This Gothic
church was designed for Bishop
George Washington Doane, whose
Italian villa by John Notman is
reproduced on page 55.*

51

ABOVE: *Kingscote, Residence of George Noble Jones, Newport, Rhode Island, 1838 (Richard Upjohn)*. BELOW: *Oaklands, Residence of R. H. Gardiner, Gardiner, Maine, 1835–36 (Richard Upjohn). The Gardiner castle was Upjohn's first significant commission. Kingscote was built for Gardiner's son-in-law. Note wing on the left of Kingscote. This was added by McKim, Mead & White in 1880. An interior view of the McKim, Mead & White wing is reproduced on page 93.*

ABOVE: *Whalers' Church, Sag Harbor, New York, 1844(Minard Lafever)*.
BELOW: *Masonic Temple, Sag Harbor, New York, 1845(Minard Lafever)*. *Lafever, a self-made architect who was once a carpenter, was responsible for the rich
Gothic Church of Holy Trinity on Brooklyn Heights, New York. He also published five handbooks for the guidance of builders. He was versatile, as may be
seen from the contrast of the Grecian Masonic Temple with the vaguely Egyptian
Whalers' Church.*

THE DEAD SHALL BE RAISED.

Grove Street Cemetery, New Haven, Connecticut, 1845–46 (Henry Austin). The Egyptian style was favored for the entrances of cemeteries, although one angry critic dismissed Egyptian architecture as fit for "embalmed cats and deified crocodiles."

Residence of Rt. Rev. George Washington Doane, Burlington, New Jersey, 1837 (John Notman). Presumably the first Italian villa erected in the United States.

ABOVE: *Second Bank of the United States, Philadelphia, Pennsylvania, 1818–24(William Strickland).* BELOW: *Merchants' Exchange, Philadelphia, Pennsylvania, 1832–34(William Strickland). Philadelphia was one of the great centers of the Greek Revival, and one of the leading Philadelphia architects was William Strickland who later designed the Grecian Capitol of Tennessee.*

Residence of Elias Brown, Old Mystic, Connecticut, 1835 (architect unknown).

Mitchell-Turner house, Milan, Ohio, c. 1828 (architect unknown).

57

Girard College, Philadelphia, Pennsylvania, 1833(Thomas U. Walter).

58

OPPOSITE ABOVE: *Andalusia, Residence of Nicholas Biddle, Andalusia, Pennsylvania, 1833(Thomas U. Walter & Nicholas Biddle).* ABOVE: *River Temple at Andalusia.* OPPOSITE BELOW: *Drawing Room, Andalusia.*

Usually remembered as the indomitable adversary of Andrew Jackson, Biddle was more than just the president of the Second Bank of the United States. "The two great truths of the world," he announced, "are the Bible and Grecian architecture." His own home, planned with the aid of Thomas Ustick Walter, who later completed the dome of the U.S. Capitol, was modeled after the Theseum at Athens. Biddle fought and won the good fight for the Grecian structure of Girard College. He announced, when victory was near, that "for the first time since Pericles architecture was introduced into city politics."

Oak Alley, Vacherie, Louisiana, c. 1836 (architect unknown). This was built for the planter J. T. Roman, brother of the Louisiana Governor André Roman.

Belle Grove, White Castle, Louisiana, 1857 (Henry Howard). This majestic ruin was leveled by fire after this negative was taken. The original owner was the planter John Andrews, Jr.

ABOVE: *Belle Meade, Residence of William Giles Harding, Nashville, Tennessee, 1853(William Strickland).* BELOW: *Gaineswood, Residence of Nathan Bryan Whitfield, Demopolis, Alabama, 1842(architect unknown).*

Ruins of Windsor Plantation, Port Gibson, Mississippi, 1861 (architect unknown).

ABOVE: *Afton Villa, Residence of David Barrow, Saint Francisville, Louisiana,* *1849(architect unknown).* BELOW: *Staunton Hill, Residence of Charles Bruce,* *Charlotte County, Virginia, 1848(John Johnson).*

Longwood, Residence of Haller Nutt, Natchez, Mississippi, 1860 (Samuel Sloan). This example of what might be termed a Moorish Revival was left uncompleted when the Civil War interrupted the owner's ambition. The architect was a Philadelphian who published a builders' guide.

Rattle & Snap, Residence of George Polk, Columbia, Tennessee,
1845 (architect unknown).

Greenwood, Residence of William Ruffin Barrow, Saint Francis-ville, Louisiana, c. 1830(architect unknown).

Church of the Cross, Bluffton, South Carolina, 1854 (E. B. White).
The architect of this unfinished-cypress Gothic church had a real
feeling for texture. He would have been at ease in twentieth-century
California.

OPPOSITE ABOVE: *Berry Hill, Residence of James Coles Bruce, Halifax County,*
Virginia, 1845 (architect unknown). BELOW: *Temple at Berry Hill.*

Stone Temple, Quincy, Massachusetts, 1828 (Alexander Parris). In the crypt of this church are buried Presidents John and John Quincy Adams.

Capitol, Columbus, Ohio, 1838–1860(Henry Walters et al).

"Wedding Cake" house, Kennebunk, Maine, c. 1800,
Gothic decoration added c. 1850(architect unknown).

OPPOSITE ABOVE: *Residence of Erastus Corning, Guilderland, New*
York, c. 1840(architect unknown). BELOW: *"The Three Bricks,"*
Nantucket, Massachusetts, 1837(architect unknown).

Grand Union Hotel, Saratoga, New York, 1872(architect unknown). This example of the mansardic style was destroyed shortly after this picture was taken.

During and after the Civil War our architects were not certain of which way to turn. The mansardic style, modeled after that of Paris in the Second Empire, was popular, and an attempt was made to propagate the Venetian Gothic advocated by John Ruskin in England. Many buildings in the Age of Indecision were brutal and confused, but only a snob could fail to recognize and admire the vitality of much of American architecture at this time.

Residence of Webster Wagner, Palatine Bridge, New York, 1877 (architect unknown). This specimen of the mansardic style was the home of Webster Wagner, the inventor of the sleeping cars in use on the Vanderbilt-owned New York Central system.

75

THE AGE OF INDECISION

ABOVE: *Olana, Residence of F. E. Church, Greendale-on-Hudson, New York, 1872 (F. E. Church & Calvert Vaux). Olana was the villa of one of the most successful romantic painters, a master of panoramas of volcanoes in Central America. Church was aided by Calvert Vaux, an architect who helped lay out Central Park in New York.* BELOW: *Farmers' and Mechanics' Bank, Albany, New York, 1876 (Russell Sturgis). The designer of the Albany bank was one of the most loyal disciples of John Ruskin.*

Hotel del Coronado, Coronado, California, 1886–88 (Reid & Reid).

Dining Room, Hotel del Coronado.

Residence of E. J. "Lucky" Baldwin, Arcadia, California, c. 1875 (architect unknown).

OPPOSITE ABOVE: *Residence of William Carson, Eureka, California, c. 1885 (architect unknown).* BELOW: *Vestibule, Residence of William Carson, Eureka, California, c. 1885 (architect unknown).*

79

H. H. RICHARDSON

Henry Hobson Richardson, a native of Louisiana who graduated from Harvard College and studied at the École des Beaux Arts, was the genius who brought order to American architecture after the Civil War. The victim of a disease which cursed him with the waistline of a hippopotamus, he ate and drank with the bravery of a man who was well aware of his own death sentence, and he advertised his disdain for death by wearing bright yellow waistcoats.

The sculptor Augustus Saint-Gaudens, who knew and worshipped Richardson, has written that "although afflicted with a trouble for which he was absolutely prohibited stimulants, he once drank a quart of black coffee when on his way to Pittsburgh, in order to be in good condition when he met the committee to arrange for the building of that masterpiece, the jail and courthouse.

"At any rate, whenever I visited (him) . . . he would say before dinner: 'S-S-Saint-Gaudens, ordinarily I lead a life of abstinence, but tonight I am going to break my rule to celebrate your visit, you come so rarely.' He would thereupon order a magnum of champagne which, as none of the family drank it, had to be finished by him and me. . . . This had to be accompanied by cheese, which was also proscribed by the doctor, and of this he ate enormous quantities. The proceeding doubtless occurred every night, as he always managed to bring home a guest."

"There is a lot of work to do, isn't there?" Richardson once asked. "And *such* work! And to think that I may die here in this office at any moment." There were friends who marveled at the schooners of iced beer he downed in Venice, and declared that he would "never take the time to die." But he died on April 27, 1886, when not yet forty-eight. "The things I want most to design," he once protested, "are a grain elevator and the interior of a great river steamboat." He designed neither of these things, but he worked his will on American architecture as have few men before or since.

Trinity Church, Boston, Massachusetts, 1872–77. Superficially Ro-
manesque in inspiration, Trinity Church was one of the great monu-
ments of the 19th century. That a building could be so carefully
composed was a lesson for the architects of the Age of Indecision.
The porch was added in the 1890's by Richardson's successors,
Shepley, Rutan & Coolidge.

City Hall, Albany, New York, 1880–81.

Residence of W. Watts Sherman, Newport, Rhode Island, 1874–76.
The greatest of all Richardson's domestic designs was this house for
William Watts Sherman, whose father had been a partner in the
banking house of Duncan, Sherman & Co. In 1960 it houses an Old
People's Home of the Baptist Church.

84

Ames Monument, Laramie, Wyoming, 1879. The Ames family of North Easton, Massachusetts were the greatest patrons of the architect. This is the monument he designed in memory of Oakes Ames and his brother Oliver Ames, Jr., who together financed the building of the Union Pacific Railroad. The sculptor Augustus Saint-Gaudens collaborated with the architect.

OPPOSITE ABOVE: *Oakes Ames Memorial Library, North Easton, Massachusetts, 1877–79.* BELOW: *Fireplace, Oakes Ames Memorial Library, North Easton, Massachusetts, 1877–79.*

Crane Memorial Library, Quincy, Massachusetts, 1880–83.

Oliver Ames, Jr., Memorial Town Hall, North Easton, Massachusetts, 1879–81.

86

Boston & Albany R. R. Station, Chestnut Hill, Massachusetts, 1884.

Gate Lodge, Residence of F. L. Ames, North Easton, Massachusetts, 1880–81.

Alleghany County Court House & Jail, Pittsburgh, Pennsylvania, 1884–87.

Residence of M. F. Stoughton, Cambridge, Massachusetts, 1882–83.
Mrs. Stoughton was the mother of the historian John Fiske.

OPPOSITE BELOW: *Interior, Residence of R. T. Paine, Waltham, Massachusetts,*
1886. Robert Treat Paine was the chairman of the building committee of Trinity
Church. He was also one of the original stockholders in the Calumet & Hecla
copper mines.

WILLIAM APPLETON POTTER

Saint Mary's Church, Tuxedo Park, New York, 1885. One of the most talented of Richardson's disciples was William Appleton Potter, son of Bishop Alonzo Potter of the Protestant Episcopal Church, and brother of Bishop Henry Codman Potter.

MCKIM, MEAD & WHITE

One of the great events in the history of American architecture was the formation in 1879 of the firm of McKim, Mead & White. Charles Follen McKim, who had studied at Harvard and at the École des Beaux Arts, was trained in the office of H. H. Richardson, as was his partner Stanford White. William Rutherford Mead, the brother-in-law of William Dean Howells, was an Amherst graduate who traveled to Florence after getting his first training in the office of the Ruskinian Gothicist Russell Sturgis.

McKim, Mead & White began their career by designing a number of summer homes and casinos for summer resorts. Usually shingle-sheathed, these have weathered out the decades so gracefully that no one can doubt that their creators were supremely sensitive to the nature of materials. This is another way of saying that McKim, Mead & White in their early work must be numbered among the great modern architects.

ABOVE: *Stables, Residence of Cyrus Hall McCormick.* BELOW: *Residence of Cyrus Hall McCormick, Richfield Springs, New York, 1882.*

MCKIM, MEAD & WHITE

Dining Room, Kingscote, Newport, Rhode Island, 1880. This typical early McKim, Mead & White interior was an addition to the Gothic cottage designed by Richard Upjohn in 1838. The exterior of the cottage is reproduced on page 52.

OPPOSITE ABOVE: *Courtyard, Newport Casino, Newport, Rhode Island, 1881.* BELOW: *Exterior, Newport Casino. Like the Cyrus Hall McCormick house, the Newport Casino may be attributed to Stanford White, whose genius as a decorator could not be denied. Since this photograph was taken the Casino has been severely damaged by fire.*

Residence of Isaac Bell, Jr., Newport, Rhode Island, 1883. Bell was the brother-in-law of James Gordon Bennett, Jr., of The New York Herald, *for whom the firm of McKim, Mead & White created the Herald Building on Herald Square. Bennett was also the founder of the Newport Casino. Stanford White was the partner in charge of the Bell house.*

Residence of C. J. Osborn, Mamaroneck, New York, 1885. Stanford White was the partner responsible for this commission. The owner was the confidential broker of Jay Gould.

Casino, Short Hills, New Jersey, 1882.

Residence of Robert Goelet, Newport, Rhode Island, 1883. Very likely Stanford White was responsible for the Casino and the Goelet mansion, both of which bear the mark of his decorative genius.

96

Residence of W. G. Low, Bristol, Rhode Island, 1887. This, the most simple, and perhaps the most noble of all the early houses of the firm, must be attributed to McKim.

A revolution in American architecture occurred on the evening of March 26, 1883, when Mr. and Mrs. W. K. Vanderbilt gave their never-to-be-forgotten ball in their new and noble château by Richard Morris Hunt on the northwest corner of Fifth Avenue and 52nd Street, New York City. The château, now destroyed, proved that a millionaire could be superbly housed in a French Renaissance design.

This was a challenge that McKim, Mead & White could not ignore. Their answer was the finest house (or rather, houses) ever built in New York City: the complex of five adjoining mansions completed in 1885 for the railroad financier Henry Villard and four of his friends. Still standing on the east side of Madison Avenue between 50th and 51st Streets, the Villard mansions marked an abrupt reversal of the approach of McKim, Mead & White. The originality and spontaneity of the shingle style was discarded in favor of a return to the Renaissance for inspiration. But let no one think that the partners in their best work were dealers in second hand goods. In this instance the Cancelleria in Rome served as a model, but it would be silly to think of the Villard mansions as a copy. Rather, this was a palace re-created in the Renaissance style for the needs of an American millionaire and his associates. The draftsman Joseph M. Wells is said to have suggested this new trend, but Stanford White was the partner in charge. From this time forward McKim, Mead & White were famous for their reinterpretations of the Renaissance for American use.

Confronted with the two splendid achievements here shown, America surrendered to McKim, Mead & White, which became the most influential firm in the history of American architecture.

The Boston Public Library, Boston, Massachusetts, 1887. This was McKim's triumph, as the Villard houses were Stanford White's. It was inspired by the Italianate Bibliothèque Sainte-Geneviève in Paris, completed by Henri Labrouste in 1850, but again was no copy.

The northern wing of the Villard complex, New York City, 1885, occupied in 1960 by the publishing firm of Random House.

The clock on the stairs of the southernmost house in the Villard complex, New York City, 1885. Originally occupied by Villard, later by Whitelaw Reid, it serves in 1960 as headquarters of the Archdiocese of New York. Stanford White here collaborated with the sculptor Augustus Saint-Gaudens.

ABOVE: *Exterior, Residence of E. D. Morgan, Wheatley Hills, Long Island, New York, 1891.* BELOW: *Courtyard, Residence of E. D. Morgan, Wheatley Hills, Long Island, New York, 1891. Since these photographs were taken, the Morgan house at Wheatley Hills has been remodeled to serve the needs of several families. Like the Morgan house at Newport, it must be attributed to McKim.*

ABOVE: *Entrance, and* BELOW: *Far view, Residence of E. D. Morgan,*
Newport, Rhode Island, 1891.

Four views of the Residence of Herman Oelrichs, Newport, Rhode Island, 1902.
ABOVE: *Grand view;* BELOW: *Closeup;* OPPOSITE ABOVE: *Front hall;* BELOW: *Ball-
room. Stanford White was responsible for this evocation of the Grand Trianon at
Versailles.*

Residence of James L. Breese, Southampton, Long Island, New York, 1906. This was one of Stanford White's last designs. In 1960 it is a center for studies in economics for Amherst College.

OPPOSITE ABOVE: *Ruins of Residence of H. A. C. Taylor, Newport, Rhode Island, 1886.* BELOW: *Germantown Cricket Club, Philadelphia, Pennsylvania, 1891. Possibly McKim was responsible for the Taylor mansion. Now destroyed, it inaugurated the Colonial Revival—which could not be long delayed, since the Renaissance, to which the partners returned again and again for inspiration, had moulded the architecture of the American colonies in the 18th century. McKim was obviously the partner who created the austere Germantown Cricket Club.*

105

Richard Morris Hunt, the first American graduate of the École des Beaux Arts, was also the first American to solve the problem of the millionaire's home. The château he completed in New York City in 1881 for Mr. and Mrs. W. K. Vanderbilt—now destroyed—proved that the early French Renaissance was a congenial setting for the masters of America's new fortunes. The success of the W. K. Vanderbilt château sent McKim, Mead & White to the Renaissance for the inspiration of their later work.

The Breakers, which was one of Hunt's many expensive commissions, was planned for the grandson of Commodore Vanderbilt, founder of the New York Central System.

ABOVE: *The Breakers, Residence of Cornelius Vanderbilt II, Newport, Rhode Island, 1892–95;* BELOW: *Dining Room, The Breakers;* OPPOSITE: *Great Hall, The Breakers. This palace in the manner of 16th century Genoa is now open to the public.*

Marble House, Residence of Mr. and Mrs. W. K. Vanderbilt, Newport, Rhode Island, 1893–95. Behind this Corinthian colonnade Mrs. Vanderbilt plotted the marriage of her daughter Consuelo to the ninth Duke of Marlborough.

ABOVE: *East view, Ochre Court, Residence of Ogden Goelet, New-port, Rhode Island, 1889–91.* BELOW: *West view. For this, perhaps the most successful of all his mansions, Hunt turned again to the early French Renaissance which had already inspired the W. K. Vanderbilt château in New York City. In 1960 Ochre Court is occupied by Salve Regina College.*

Drawing Room, Ochre Court, Residence of Ogden Goelet,
Newport, Rhode Island, 1889–91.

Biltmore, Residence of George Washington Vanderbilt II, Asheville, North Carolina, 1895. Biltmore, Henry James confessed, was "a thing of the high Rothschild manner." It was built for the brother of Cornelius Vanderbilt II and W. K. Vanderbilt.

CHARLES ADAMS PLATT

Residence of John Jay Chapman, Barrytown, New York, 1914(Charles Adams Platt). Platt was an eminent rival of McKim, Mead & White. A sensitive student of the Renaissance, he designed this house for Stanford White's friend and admirer, the critic John Jay Chapman.

HORACE TRUMBAUER

Miramar, Residence of A. Hamilton Rice, Newport, Rhode Island, 1916(Horace Trumbauer). Horace Trumbauer was famous as the architect for the Widener family of Philadelphia. Mrs. Rice had previously been married to George Dunton Widener, and the Widener Library at Harvard—in memory of her son who went down on the Titanic—*was entrusted to the Trumbauer firm. Trumbauer is known to have stayed far away from the drafting room of his office. Miramar was probably designed by his draftsman Julian Abele, a gifted Negro who was obviously fond of the work of the great eighteenth century master Jacques-Ange Gabriel.*

ABOVE: *Entrance,* BELOW: *Closeup, Hotel Ponce de León, Saint Augustine, Florida, 1885–88. Bernard R. Maybeck, later one of the great architects of California, was in the Carrère & Hastings office at this time, and to him has been attributed the vivacity of this hotel. It was planned for H. M. Flagler, the first to appreciate Florida's possibilities as a winter resort.*

De Vinne Press Building, New York City, 1885. This was one of the great commercial buildings of New York City in the days when Hunt and McKim, Mead & White were building their great palaces. In its austerity, the De Vinne Press Building owes much to the example of H. H. Richardson.

JOHN & WASHINGTON ROEBLING

Brooklyn Bridge, Brooklyn, New York, 1867–83. The greatest engineering achievement of the 19th century, this was completed in the very year that Mr. and Mrs. W. K. Vanderbilt moved into their new château on Fifth Avenue.

Too easily dismissed as the coiner of the unfortunate slogan "Form follows function," Louis Henri Sullivan was no mechanical functionalist, but an artist who understood that every successful building was the solution of a unique problem. With his partner Dankmar Adler, whose grasp of engineering and acoustics went unrivalled, Sullivan designed The Auditorium, a complex that included a hotel and the world's most distinguished opera house. The late Samuel Insull was responsible for the closing of the opera house and the removal of the Chicago Opera Company to a building he financed on the Chicago River. In 1960 the Auditorium houses Roosevelt University, which has launched a campaign to restore the opera house to its old usefulness and grandeur.

OPPOSITE: *The Auditorium, Chicago, Illinois, 1889.*
ABOVE: *Interior, The Auditorium.*

Decorative panel, The Guaranty Building. Sullivan was also a genius at the art of decoration, an art that has been overlooked by the contrivers of the skyscrapers in our own time.

ADLER & SULLIVAN

The Guaranty Building, Buffalo, New York, 1895.
As a designer of skyscrapers, Louis Sullivan has never been equalled.

*Carson, Pirie Scott & Company Building, Chicago, Illinois, 1899.
Now occupied by the department store of Carson, Pirie Scott &
Company, this building was planned for the firm of Schlesinger &
Mayer. Dankmar Adler had withdrawn from the partnership by
the time this commission was executed.*

120

Closeup, Carson, Pirie Scott & Company Building, Chicago, Illinois, 1899. Sullivan's faithful friend George Grant Elmslie is known to have sketched the ornamental work on this building.

Merchants' National Bank, Grinnell, Iowa, 1914. Depressed by the emphasis of the Chicago World's Fair of 1893 on the classical revival, Sullivan watched his practice dwindle in his last years. But there was no decline in the quality of his work.

Tomb of Carrie Eliza Getty, Graceland Cemetery, Chicago, Illinois, 1890.

LOUIS SULLIVAN

National Farmers' Bank, Owatonna, Minnesota, 1907–08. Sullivan's associate George Grant Elmslie is known to have assisted him on this masterpiece. Since this photograph was taken, the bank has been enlarged and restored by Harwell Hamilton Harris. In his restoration Harris has displayed a total understanding of Sullivan's aims.

ABOVE: *Residence of H. C. Bradley, Woods Hole, Massachusetts, 1912.* BELOW: *Interior of living room. In its adaptation to the site, and in its emphasis on the nature of materials, this seaside cottage recalls the great achievements of the early days of McKim, Mead & White. The firm of Purcell & Elmslie, which flourished in Chicago and Minneapolis in the early twentieth century, was formed by William Gray Purcell, a devoted admirer of Louis Sullivan, and George Grant Elmslie, Sullivan's friend to the end.*

125

Mechants National Bank, Winona, Minnesota, 1911.
George Feick was a partner in the firm when this bank was designed.

126

Residence of J. G. Melson, Mason City, Iowa, 1913. The designer of this house was one of the challenging architects of the Middle West in the early twentieth century. Trained in the office of Frank Lloyd Wright, Griffin won the international competition for the plan of Canberra, the capital of Australia, and spent his last years in Australia and India. Since this photograph was taken, the Melson house has been altered out of recognition.

GUENZEL & DRUMMOND

River Forest Women's Club, River Forest, Illinois, 1913. William Drummond of the firm of Guenzel & Drummond was also trained in the office of Frank Lloyd Wright.

Unity Temple, Oak Park, Illinois, 1906.

The most inventive and probably the greatest of all American architects was Sullivan's pupil Frank Lloyd Wright, who fought a lifelong battle for what he termed "organic architecture." A building, he held, should grow easily from its site and be designed from inside out. A champion of informal planning, he decided that walls should be screens instead of barriers. He also emphasized, with uncanny sympathy, the texture of whatever materials he used.

Wright was always aware of his own importance. He understood, as did no one else, that the wistful artist is no artist at all.

Residence of Susan Lawrence Dana, Springfield, Illinois, 1903.

Residence of B. Harley Bradley, Kankakee, Illinois, 1900.

Playhouse for the children of Avery Coonley, Riverside, Illinois, 1912.

The Bradley house has been preserved as a restaurant, but the Coonley house has been altered out of recognition to be a home for five families. Even the playhouse for the Coonley children has been made over since this photograph was taken.

Residence of George Madison Millard, Pasadena, California, 1923.

Residence of Aline Barnsdall, Hollywood, California, 1920.

Two views of the Residence of R. L. Jones, Tulsa, Oklahoma, 1929.

OPPOSITE ABOVE *and* ABOVE: *Falling Water, Residence of E. J. Kauf-mann, Bear Run, Pennsylvania, 1936.* BELOW: *Interior, living room, Falling Water.*

OPPOSITE ABOVE: *Far view, Taliesin East, Residence of Frank Lloyd Wright, Spring Green, Wisconsin, 1925–59;* BELOW: *Entrance, Taliesin East;* ABOVE: *Interior, Studio, Taliesin East. Wright once observed that "no house should ever be* on *any hill or* on *anything. It should be* of *the hill, belonging to it, so hill and house should live together each the happier for the other."*

ABOVE: *Courtyard, Taliesin East, Residence of Frank Lloyd Wright,*
Spring Green, Wisconsin, 1925–59; BELOW: *Mrs. Wright's wing, Taliesin East.*

FRANK LLOYD WRIGHT

ABOVE: *Office, Taliesin West, Residence of Frank Lloyd Wright,
Phoenix, Arizona, 1938–59.* BELOW: *Terrace, Taliesin West.*

ABOVE: *Drafting room, Taliesin West, Residence of Frank Lloyd Wright,*
Phoenix, Arizona, 1938–59. BELOW: *Interior, Living room, Taliesin West.*

Research Tower, S. C. Johnson & Son, Racine, Wisconsin, 1951.

Interior and exterior, Administration Building, S. C. Johnson & Son, Racine, Wisconsin, 1939.

Exterior and interior, First Unitarian Meeting House, Madison, Wisconsin, 1951.

ABOVE: *Entrance Lodge and* BELOW: *Main House, Auldbrass Plantation, Residence of Leigh Stevens, Yemassee, South Carolina, 1940.*

FRANK LLOYD WRIGHT

Closeup and full view, V. C. Morris Store,
San Francisco, California, 1949.

FRANK LLOYD WRIGHT

The most remarkable campus to be laid out since Thomas Jefferson's University of Virginia is Florida Southern College.

Administration Building, Florida Southern College, Lakeland, Florida, 1948.

ABOVE: *Pfeiffer Chapel, Florida Southern College, Lakeland, Florida, 1940.*

BELOW: *Roux Library, Florida Southern College, Lakeland, Florida, 1942.*

Residence of Lowell Walter, Quasqueton, Iowa, 1949.

Boat house for Lowell Walter, Quasqueton, Iowa, 1949.

H. C. Price Tower, Bartlesville, Oklahoma, 1955.

Interior of the Central Hall, and two views of the exterior,
Guggenheim Museum, New York City, 1959.

Residence of Mrs. Clinton Walker, Carmel, California, 1952.

Residence of David Wright, Phoenix, Arizona, 1952.

IRVING GILL

Residence of Miss Ellen Scripps, La Jolla, California, 1914.

If modern architects may be divided into two classes, those whose approach is impersonal and those whose approach is personal, Gill obviously belongs with the first group. In his disdain of all decoration he was close to the Viennese Adolf Loos. Like Frank Lloyd Wright, Gill was a graduate of Louis Sullivan's office.

Since this photograph was taken, the Scripps house has been remodeled by the local art museum which makes use of the building, and few traces remain of the architect's intentions. Gill was, however, one of the important architects of California in the early twentieth century, and before the remodeling was carried out this was one of his important buildings.

Residence of W. D. Tremaine, Santa Barbara, California, 1948.

Neutra is famous for the impersonal elegance of his designs. A graduate of the office of Adolf Loos in his native Vienna, Neutra settled in Los Angeles in 1925 after an apprenticeship with Erich Mendelsohn in Berlin and Holabird & Roche in Chicago.

OPPOSITE ABOVE: *Residence of Marcel Breuer, Lincoln, Massachusetts, 1939 (Gropius & Breuer).* BELOW: *Residence of Gilbert Tompkins, Hewlett Harbor, Long Island, New York, 1946 (Marcel Breuer).*

WALTER GROPIUS

MARCEL BREUER

Walter Gropius, who headed the Bauhaus, a school of architecture and design in Weimar and Dessau in his native Germany, was made head of the Harvard School of Architecture in 1937. His most recent work has been as a consultant for the New York builder-architects Emery Roth & Sons.

An impersonal educator in Germany and in America, he has insisted that "collective architectural work becomes possible only when every individual, prepared by proper schooling, is capable of understanding the idea of the whole, and thus has the means harmoniously to co-ordinate his independent, even if limited activity with the collective work."

Marcel Breuer, who taught both at the Bauhaus and at Harvard, is in 1960, like Gropius, engaged in independent practice.

Apartment House at 860 Lake Shore Drive, Chicago, Illinois, 1951.

LUDWIG MIËS VAN DER ROHE

Residence of Philip Johnson, New Canaan, Connecticut, 1948.

A brilliant propagandist for the architecture of Walter Gropius and Ludwig Miës van der Rohe, Johnson went into the profession after establishing himself as a critic. He was recently associated with Miës in the design of the Seagram Building, New York City.

A graduate of the office of Peter Behrens in Berlin, Miës headed the Bauhaus at Dessau after the resignation of Walter Gropius. He has been true to the ideal he set for himself in 1924. "The whole trend of our time," he then wrote, "is toward the secular. The endeavors of the mystics will be remembered as mere episodes. Despite our greater understanding of life, we shall build no cathedrals. Nor do the brave gestures of the romantics mean anything to us, for behind them we detect the empty form. . . . The individual is losing significance; his destiny is no longer what interests us. The decisive achievements in all fields are impersonal, and their authors are for the most part obscure. They are part of the trend of our times toward anonymity."

157

WALLACE K. HARRISON

United Nations Secretariat, New York City, 1950 (Wallace K. Harrison & Associates). The influence of the famous Swiss architect Le Corbusier is unmistakable in this building. Impersonal in most of his work, Le Corbusier has only recently experimented with sculptural forms in which his personality is evident.

SKIDMORE, OWINGS
& MERRILL

ABOVE: *Lever House, New York City, 1952.* BELOW: *Manufacturers' Trust Building, New York City, 1954. The giant firm of Skidmore, Owings & Merrill owes much to the meticulous example of Ludwig Miës van der Rohe.*

159

MINORU YAMASAKI

McGregor Memorial, Wayne University, Detroit, Michigan, 1958(Yamasaki, Leinweber & Associates). Minoru Yamasaki is a native of Seattle. The lyrical accuracy of his mind is evident in this new building for the Wayne campus.

PIETRO BELLUSCHI

OPPOSITE ABOVE: *Equitable Building, Portland, Oregon, 1948(Pietro Belluschi). To the right of the Equitable Building may be seen the U.S. National Bank Building designed by the firm of A. K. Doyle in 1917. Belluschi was for many years a member of the Doyle firm.*

JOHN YEON

OPPOSITE BELOW: *Residence of A. R. Watsek, Portland, Oregon, 1938(John Yeon). Yeon was associated with Belluschi at the time he designed this sensitive frame house.*

MINORU YAMASAKI

*Far view and closeup, Municipal Airport, Saint Louis, Missouri, 1954
(Yamasaki, Leinweber & Associates).*

Closeup, David S. Ingalls Hockey Rink, Yale University, New Haven, Connecticut, 1959(Eero Saarinen & Associates).

The son of the late Eliel Saarinen, who designed Cranbrook School at Bloomfield Hills, Michigan, Eero Saarinen is one of the commanding figures of twentieth century architecture. He solves engineering problems with such ease that it may be said that he provides answers for questions not yet asked.

*Far view and interior, David S. Ingalls Hockey Rink,
Yale University, New Haven, Connecticut, 1959
(Eero Saarinen & Associates).*

Interior, Styling Building, General Motors Technical Center, Warren, Michigan, 1952(Eero Saarinen & Associates).

Closeup and far view, Styling Building, General Motors Technical Center, Warren, Michigan, 1952 (Eero Saarinen & Associates). The sculpture is the work of Antoine Pevsner.

Palace of Fine Arts, San Francisco, California, 1915. This master-piece from the Panama-Pacific Exposition was created by a graduate of the École des Beaux Arts who worked in the office of Carrère & Hastings before moving to California. "The keynote of a Fine Arts Palace," Maybeck claimed, "should be that of sadness, modified by the feeling that beauty has a soothing influence. . . . Great ex-amples of melancholy in architecture and gardens may be seen in the engravings of Piranesi . . . whose remarkable work conveys the sad minor notes of old Roman ruins covered with bushes and trees."

167

First Church of Christ Scientist, and interior, Berkeley, California, 1912. This church suggests that there may be more to modern architecture than glass walls and steel frames.

Residence of Charles M. Pratt, Ojai, California, c. 1910.

The brothers Charles Sumner and Henry Mather Greene were natives of
Saint Louis. After graduating from the Manual Training School of Washington University and the Massachusetts Institute of Technology, they settled
in Southern California and made it plain that no one was more expert than
they in emphasizing the texture of timber.

Residence of David B. Gamble, Pasadena, California, 1909.

*Exterior and living room, Residence of Harry Weese, Barrington, Illinois, 1958.
The cordial informality of the architect's own house proves that he would be
entirely at home in the undoctrinaire world of San Francisco.*

Residence of C. H. Wolfe, Catalina Island, California, 1928.

A student of Otto Wagner in his native Vienna, Schindler went to work for Frank Lloyd Wright before setting up his own office in Los Angeles. To the end of his life (he died in 1953) he fought against the impersonal gospel of Walter Gropius and Miës van der Rohe.

HARWELL HAMILTON HARRIS

Residence of Clarence Wyle, Ojai, California, 1948.

Harris is the Californian who has given new meaning to the great tradition of Maybeck and the brothers Greene & Greene.

Exterior and living room, Residence of Weston Havens, Berkeley, California, 1941. One of the great houses of the twentieth century, it commands but does not dictate to, an amazing view of San Francisco and the Bay and Golden Gate Bridges.

HARWELL HAMILTON HARRIS

Residence of Ralph Johnson, Los Angeles, California, 1949.

OPPOSITE: *Exterior and interior, Residence of J. S. Treanor, Abilene, Texas, 1959.*
Harris has recently established his office in Dallas.

Offices of Schuckl & Company, Canners, Sunnyvale, California, 1942.

WILLIAM WILSON WURSTER

In Wurster's eyes, the designer of a house enjoys a rare privilege. "Families heading for the divorce courts don't build houses," he has said. "Houses are built by husbands and wives in the happiest period of their lives, and architects, unlike lawyers or doctors, have to be thankful that they are dealing with optimists."

Residence of I. Schuman, Woodside, California, 1949.

"There is," says William Wilson Wurster, "always more than one answer." He has never been dogmatic. This may be one reason for the enormous practice of the firm of Wurster, Bernardi & Emmons which he founded in 1945. Formerly head of the School of Architecture at the Massachusetts Institute of Technology, in 1960 he directs the School of Architecture at the University of California at Berkeley.

177

Center for Advanced Study in the Behavioral Sciences, Palo Alto, California, 1954. ABOVE: *Exterior;* OPPOSITE BELOW: *Library;* ABOVE: *Dining Room.* The Center is only one of many examples of Wurster's skill in blending a building with its site.

INDEX (ARCHITECTS IN ITALICS)